VOGUE ON

JEAN PAUL GAULTIER

Carolyn Asome

quadrille

Portrait of Jean Paul Gaultier by Peter Lindbergh, showing the serious side of the designer, whose rigorous couture training provided a powerful foundation for the drama of his clothes.

Page 1 *Bold, geometric and architectural corsetry reimagined for the 21st century: Malgosia Bela in Gaultier's Mongolian-wool coat and gold and silver lamé corset from the autumn/winter 2009 couture collection,* Les Actrices. *Photograph by Josh Olins.*

Previous page *Natalia Vodianova wears an embroidered, tailored peplum dress, opened to expose lingerie beneath. Photograph by Mario Testino.*

'I BECAME FASCINATED WITH THE
IDEA OF TRANSFORMING ONE'S
BODY WITH CLOTHES.'

JEAN PAUL GAULTIER

REBEL IN A CORSET

As a sobriquet, *enfant terrible* might not seem appropriate for a man in his mid-60s but, for Jean Paul Gaultier, that epithet still seems fitting. Though his once dyed platinum-blonde hair is now turning an ashy grey, the maverick designer is still impish, and the considerable body of work he has produced, in a career that has spanned 40 years, has consistently pushed the boundaries of good taste. Drawing upon the counterculture for inspiration, Gaultier has trampled on convention, though not indiscriminately. According to Lionel Vermeil, his press officer for twenty years, 'If something is a tradition, he doesn't touch it. If it's a convention, he pulverizes it.'

Not many fashion designers become household names. Fewer still become household faces. And yet Jean Paul Gaultier has managed both. In 1976 he launched his own collection, rustled up from upholstery fabric with tin cans for bracelets. Ever since, he has demonstrated a willingness to break taboos and challenge the status quo, with skirts and make-up for men, or lingerie worn as outerwear on waspish Parisiennes and corseted geishas, or Tyrolean maidens in bomber jackets and blonde plaits. He has invaded our screens as the lively presenter of cult TV programme *Eurotrash*, launched a sublime, flourishing couture line and created a globally successful perfume.

Ever inventive, his immense talent (and his indefatigable work ethic) has thrilled, revolutionised and entertained the fashion world, with clothes possessed of an eccentricity, daring and exuberance that have clocked up more headline-grabbing moments than those of most designers. In the pages of *Vogue*, photos of supermodels such as Linda Evangelista, and Kate Moss – captured by Herb Ritts, Bruce Weber and Peter Lindbergh – reveal Gaultier's instinct for how women wanted to dress. Gaultier set out to prove that fashion need not be elitist. From the beginning, Gaultier seemed hell-bent on democratising it, not only given that most of his inspiration came from the street but because he thought everyone – no matter who they were, where they came from, their size, shape or colour – should have access to it.

'I LIKE WHEN DREAMS BECOME REALITY BECAUSE THAT IS MY LIFE.'

JEAN PAUL GAULTIER

As a child Gaultier would listen to his grandmother tell stories about life during the Second World War. Women had to recycle then, and learn to cope with the shortages: so, for example, men's suits were altered for women and trousers became skirts. Gaultier's ideas for an 'off-beat fashion' were inspired by those stories, when deprivation forced people to be imaginative. In his case, by enriching recycled objects he made them magnificent. Sumptuous linings turned military pieces into formal attire; evening gowns were reworked from camouflage material or parachute fabric.

He has produced futuristic-looking global nomads and explored hybrid human/animal personas through the use of feathers and animal skins; these looks were also to inspire the work of his design assistant Nicolas Ghesquière as well as Alexander McQueen and John Galliano. Taking his cue from flea-market stands and Marrakesh souks, Gaultier has mixed style, colours and cultures. His collections are mash-ups that always reflect what is going on in the wider world, with their liberally sprinkled references to sex, music and everyday life. Nevertheless, although he chose to rebel against the old school of Parisian couture, owing to his years of training within its system under Pierre Cardin, Jacques Esterel and Jean Patou, he is a master craftsman. However avant-garde his collections may seem, his inventive tailoring is always technically brilliant.

At the heart of so many of his shows is an enduring affection for Paris, particularly the Paris of the interwar years. Carine Roitfeld, former editor of *Vogue Paris*, believes that he is French even more than just Parisian. 'With his sailor style sweater, practically wearing a beret – the only thing missing is a baguette under his arm! – and in the way he lives, sees things and creates. He knows our country's conventions inside out and has been able to hang on to his national identity, to avoid being sucked into the big international soup that is everywhere and nowhere.'

Yasmin Le Bon is wrapped up in Gaultier's love for pile-it-on exuberance. Like a Surrealist collagist he has thrown silk flower appliqué, tassels and jet beads onto a black jacket with red-striped sleeves, shiny stretch collar and yoke. Photograph by Peter Lindbergh

Overleaf *Sante D'Orazio captures Tatjana Patitz (left) wearing a studded black nylon body suit with golden appliqué. A fascination with jewellery and embellishment has continued throughout Gaultier's design career. Linda Evangelista (right) wears a voluminous fake cheetah-print skirt over a black tiered petticoat with black jersey top and gloves. Photograph by Hans Feurer.*

'THERE IS
SOMETHING
INEFFABLY FRENCH
ABOUT HIS
CLOTHES.'

LISA ARMSTRONG, VOGUE

Wearing his signature striped matelot sweater, Jean Paul Gaultier surveys his handiwork for his first haute couture collection, which was shown in 1997. He was only the third designer in three decades to create a couture line under his own label. Photograph by Mario Testino.

'You are a true designer when people recognise your work without even looking at the label', said Pierre Cardin of Gaultier, whom the couturier had hired on Gaultier's eighteenth birthday, though Cardin added, 'There are aspects of his designs, like his highly androgynous looks, that are not exactly my cup of tea. Also, I don't see why he stubbornly persists in putting women back into corsets. They've only just got rid of them.'

What shines through most in Gaultier's work and career is an enduring love of fashion. He told *Vogue*, 'I am not interested in business, I didn't do fashion to become rich and famous.' 'He is and always has been true to himself, he has never wavered from his aesthetic' says Lucinda Chambers, *Vogue*'s fashion director. 'What's more, he has always remained a deeply human person who touches people. The memory that sticks in my mind is when he asked a few of us in the industry – [including] Grace Coddington, Suzy Menkes, Hamish Bowles – to perform a magic show at the Olympia Theatre in Paris for his thirtieth anniversary. We had such fun. We all had our own dressing room, with posters of each of us that he had framed in the foyer, candles, food, we all felt like stars for an evening. This was such a Jean Paul kind of wonderful thing to do: involving all his favourite people and doing the thing he loved – performance and giving pleasure.'

Corseting from Les Actrices, *Gaultier's autumn/winter 2009 couture collection. His love of corsets came from his grandmother Marie Garrabe who had a wardrobe full of them, beginning an obsession with a particular way of displaying the female form that was to become his trademark. Photograph by Chris Moore.*

Jean Paul Gaultier was born on the 24th April, 1952 in Arcueil, Val-de-Marne, a suburb to the south of Paris. He was the only child of a book-keeper, Paul Gaultier, and Solange, his wife, who worked as a cashier at a school canteen. On the streets of Arcueil, the young Gaultier saw no chic women dressed in the post New Look fashion of France's great couturiers; its predominantly working-class citizens did not trail perfume clouds of elegance back from the capital. Arcueil was bleak and grey with smoke from factory chimneys rising into the air. As Gaultier was to observe later, it was where a *Nouvelle Vague* film about the grittiness of working-class life might have been filmed. His parents were hard-working, tolerant people who Gaultier's cousin

Evelyne Gaultier described as 'open-minded and considerate of others, no matter who they might be'. But it was Gaultier's maternal grandmother, Marie Garrabe, who was to exert the most lasting and powerful influence on his childhood and indeed his whole life.

He did not find it easy to make friends at school and by his own admission was happiest in his own world of make-believe. He did not enjoy football or gym like all the other boys and girls and admitted later to *Vogue* that he would invent things and lie in order to gain affection. The highlight of his week was Thursday when he would go to stay at his grandmother's house, arriving on Wednesday evening and frequently feigning sickness on Friday so that he might stretch his visit until the weekend. Garrabe indulged him and he adored her. He enjoyed her central heating (a great luxury in the Fifties) and, as he remembers it, other treats such as a fridge and television: he was spoiled and allowed to watch programmes not usually permissible for a boy his age.

A local character, Garrabe was also a mystic, hypnotist and early practitioner of alternative healing, essentially running a home beauty parlour where she would dispense advice on hair, beauty and matters of the heart. As he explained to *Women's Wear Daily*, 'From her I learned the importance of physical appearance as it related to the interior life – the importance of attitudes, gestures, movement and how everything is connected.' He was fascinated by the atmosphere in her heavy, dark rooms that were decorated with bourgeois touches of lace tablecloths, old-fashioned lamps, and equally enthralled by her clothes, hats, feathers and jewellery which dated back to the early part of the century and sparked his imagination.

Corinne Day captures a green tulle confection, decorated with silk flowers around the décolleté, in a setting that is reminiscent of Gaultier's grandmother's house with its shadowy rooms, vintage lampshades and clothes.

Overleaf *Cate Blanchett demonstrates Gaultier's couture showmanship in a black organza, ruffled, off-the-shoulder dress. It combines fin-de-siècle glamour with restrained sophistication. Photograph by Regan Cameron.*

'In the beginning, I wanted to design costumes and scenery for the Folies Bergère cabaret in Paris.'

JEAN PAUL GAULTIER

'ELEGANCE IS A QUESTION OF PERSONALITY, MORE THAN CLOTHING.'

JEAN PAUL GAULTIER

Gaultier told Susan Orlean in *The New Yorker* that when women confided that their husbands were losing interest in them, Garrabe would recommend that they 'jazz up their wardrobes', and that he was fascinated by the idea that fashion was powerful enough to save a relationship. He loved to draw and would make 'before' and 'after' sketches showing how the women might transform if they heeded his grandmother's advice, which usually meant, to him, looking like Ava Gardner or Marilyn Monroe. Gaultier remembers how she always told him positive things: '"You'll be famous and do well in life," she would say to me. I think she did it to help my confidence.' She also encouraged him to express himself creatively.

Garrabe had a wardrobe full of peach- and salmon-pink-coloured corsets; she told him that she used to drink a swig of vinegar before putting one on, so her stomach would contract and the laces could be pulled even tighter. She would ask her grandson for help lacing up the corset, and this was responsible for an obsession with the female form that was to become his trademark. 'From that moment,' he told *Vogue*, "I became fascinated by the idea of transforming one's body with clothes, and the idea that certain garments can accentuate something you want and hide something you don't.'

As Colin McDowell explains in his book *Jean Paul Gaultier*, his grandmother was his link to the popular entertainment of the past. 'She would fiddle with the radio until she found Charles Trenet singing or Maurice Chevalier, Jean Sablon or Piaf. But Gaultier also did his fiddling until he found the performers he liked, pre-eminently Françoise Hardy, whose clothes excited him as much as her voice, Juliette Greco and a vulgar but entertaining singer called Sheila.' A seminal moment in his cultural education was the first time he heard the Rolling Stones singing 'Satisfaction'. As he tells McDowell, 'It was a revelation. I didn't understand a word of it but I understood its strength. For me, I now realise, its impact was sexual.'

Unashamedly luxurious: Jean Paul Gaultier puts a glamorous spin on knitwear for the evening with this silver and gold dress with knitted top and translucent pleated taffeta skirt. Photograph by Arthur Elgort

Television also fuelled his fantasies. Which is how, one night, he chanced upon a documentary about the Folies Bergère. He was mesmerised by the glamour of the dancers in their fishnet stockings, wearing little else. At school the next morning, Gaultier sat at the back of his class drawing the women he had seen on TV. He was caught and his teacher, outraged, pinned the artwork to his back and made him parade up and down to humiliate him in front of his classmates. But the punishment backfired. 'All the boys cheered me,' Gaultier told *Vogue*. 'It was the first time they had had a positive reaction to me and I soon realised that drawing was my passport to making people smile. I became this local hero.' He was hooked and began to sketch away. Aged 12 he saw Jacques Becker's *Falbalas*, the 1945 film drama set around a Parisian haute couture house which showed how a fictional couturier walked, talked and created. For an impressionable Gaultier, it represented a glamorous world and became part of his daydreams. Spurred on by the positive reception his sketches had received he was no longer afraid to admit his passion for clothes and spectacle, and showed his family everything he drew. And even though his parents harboured hopes that he might one day become a Spanish teacher, the die was cast for him to become a fashion designer.

His teddy bear was his first model and re-lived the big stories of the day. As he told Celia Walden in the *Daily Telegraph*: 'The first cone-shaped bra I made was for that bear; the poor thing went through a lot. When the Duchess of Kent and [before that] Queen Fabiola of Belgium got married, he had to wear wedding dresses. Then the first time open heart-surgery was performed, he had to undergo that too.' The long-suffering bear is still in existence, 'but he's a catastrophe now,' laments Gaultier struggling to keep a straight face. 'You should see him: he needs silicone and Botox, the whole lot.'

Gaultier admits that it was Christian Dior and Yves Saint Laurent who made him dream. 'I really wanted to do things like they did.'

Alex Chatelain's photograph from a Vogue *shoot entitled 'The Wilder Shores of Summertime' explores the eclectic mix that was central to many of Gaultier's clothes. Here, an enormous ruffle adds a dramatic, quirky touch to a black stretch wool skirt below a black zipped top that reveals a bare midriff.*

Overleaf *Nothing escaped Gaultier's ethnic blender: here Christy Turlington as a Heidi-esque Tyrolean maid wears gloves, a Fair Isle sweater and his signature deconstructed trench coat. Photograph by Sean Cunningham.*

'I LIKE LOOKING AT THINGS FROM A DIFFERENT ANGLE AND QUESTIONING WHAT IS EXPECTED.'

JEAN PAUL GAULTIER

He devoured issues of fashion magazines like *L'Officiel* that were devoted to couture. A big turning point was when he began to design dresses for his mother; these were made up by a friend of hers and he has admitted that most of the skill in producing them was hers. Nevertheless, as McDowell says, 'His mother's willingness to indulge her son was a huge psychological fillip for his aspirations.' His parents also supported him in the notion that he might sell some of his sketches, for pocket money. An early attempt was unsuccessful: an acquaintance of his mother who worked at Dior took some of his drawings to show to Marc Bohan, the austere and classical design director at Dior who, unsurprisingly, found them too gaudy and exuberant. However, Gaultier was encouraged to send sketches to other design houses.

On the day of his eighteenth birthday in 1970 he received a call from the house of Pierre Cardin, the designer who pioneered space-age dresses, bubble skirts and the modern tunic jacket. He liked the sketches Gaultier had sent in and hired him as an assistant. Working with Pierre Cardin had a formative impact on Gaultier. Gaultier told *Vogue* that, 'Cardin was very open-minded, and even though I hadn't gone to fashion school, he believed I had talent simply on the basis of my sketches and our first meeting. He liked my ideas.' Gaultier greatly admired Cardin, who was uninterested in convention and unafraid of the *Chambre Syndicale*, the governing body of the French fashion industry. Cardin, like Yves Saint Laurent, was one of the rare couturiers who attempted to convey in his designs the spirit of the age, and he handed down to Gaultier the message that anything was possible: nothing was set in stone.

Eight months after he joined, however, it was decided that Cardin was overstaffed and, as Gaultier was the most recent hire, he was made redundant. He worked briefly with Jacques Esterel, whose fantasy ideas earned him the reputation of court jester of Paris fashion. Interestingly, as McDowell points out, in 1965 he pre-dated Gaultier's men in skirts idea with a plaid kilted suit for men and he also experimented with another Gaultier interest: trousers with zips at the back and the front.

Gaultier then worked for Jean Patou, a fusty old French house, where he was mocked for the unconventional way he had begun to dress. To his mind the house of Patou epitomised the sort of conformist and bland, bourgeois taste that he has spent the rest of his life rebelling against. He told *Vogue*, 'When I arrived one morning wearing my riding boots, the old sales ladies would say to me, "Where's your horse? Did you leave it outside?" It was not funny. Everything there was beige and gold and it was all so safe. They explained that beige and gold worn together were the shades that were the *ne plus ultra* of style but really, it depends how you put it all together.' After two years with Jean Patou, struggling to come to terms with the timidity of a fashion house still stuck firmly in the past, he returned to work for Pierre Cardin in 1974, who sent him to the Philippines to oversee Cardin's lucrative licensing deals and design collections for the American market.

Overleaf Mario Testino captures a model wearing Gaultier's mesh tube dress and leggings, which incorporate a sporty, youthful attitude. Gaultier was always as interested in young, street styles as in haute couture.

During this period in which Gaultier was finding his way, the elusive, exclusive world of haute couture was, as Farid Chenoune describes it in his 1996 Gaultier memoir, 'like a magnificent ruined city, crumbling piles of tulle, faille and organza, redolent of a past elegance and impervious to changing times, gestures and attitudes. There were rumblings in society: the oil crisis ... and on the other side of the Channel, the Sex Pistols and the punks were desecrating English brick walls with anti-social graffiti proclaiming the young generation's war-cry of "no future."'

Gaultier told *Vogue*: 'I started in couture – working with Cardin and Jean Patou – and soon appreciated that it was not my ideal métier. My affinities are with the young and unorthodox, so I create costumes that break rules, go over the top if you like.'

'Fashion must correspond to the aspirations
of the moment and reflect current events.'

JEAN PAUL GAULTIER

'MY AFFINITIES ARE
WITH THE YOUNG
AND UNORTHODOX,
SO I CREATE
COSTUMES THAT
BREAK RULES, GO
OVER THE TOP IF
YOU LIKE.'

JEAN PAUL GAULTIER

'TO CONFORM IS TO GIVE IN.'

JEAN PAUL GAULTIER

THE OUTSIDER

From the outset of his career, Gaultier was a radical, questioning every preconceived idea and frequently demolishing accepted fashion 'wisdom' with a humour and confidence that belied his 26 years. His first 'anything goes' casting sessions challenged fashion's ideals of beauty and during his design career he has always sought to embrace myriad forms of beauty – of all shapes, sizes, nationalities, ethnicities and ages. He caused shockwaves not just by celebrating the ethnically diverse, but also by hiring unconventional models: older men, full-figured women and pierced and heavily tattooed models were very much part of his catwalk shows.

The absurdity of subscribing to one ideal of beauty was anathema to the designer and was brought home to him one day in the early Seventies when he was working at Jean Patou and stumbled across a model binding her breasts flat with tape. When he asked her why she was doing that, he was stunned by her answer. 'They won't use me if I have a figure, and I need the work.' He was appalled. Nearly 30 years ago he told *Vogue*, 'You'll find beauty wherever you choose to look for it. I like difference. Perfection is relative and beauty is subjective. I wanted to make imperfection admirable. That shows in my choice of models among other things. Being homosexual and an outsider at school who didn't play football or was good at gym means I think about minorities a lot.'

In an interview with Gaby Wood in the *Observer*, he wonders if he set out to shock: 'Was I conscious of the fact that it (using normal people) could be shocking? Yes. But I just wanted to show what I found fair or normal or beautiful. If anything, I was the one who was shocked, by certain kinds of intolerance.'

A model wears a blue-and-silver panelled chiffon spotted dress with long suede waistcoat and satin headdress. Gaultier liked to use models of all ethnicities: the stereotypical, Amazonian or Nordic figure left him cold. Photograph by Paolo Roversi.

Overleaf Patrick Demarchelier captures Gaultier's frothy peach-pink skirt suit with its outré layers of taffeta and ruched, tasselled silk (left). The outfit is toughened up with a pair of Dr Martens boots, a nod to the punk phenomenon that has influenced much of his work. Gaultier's love of rock and punk influences include the liberal use of animal print through many of his collections, including this fake cheetah jacket with puffed taffeta sleeves (right). Photograph by Hans Feurer.

'It is beautiful to be what you are.'

JEAN PAUL GAULTIER

The profound love and respect he had for his grandmother meant he appreciated older people. He told *Actuel* back in 1990 that, 'Jeans become better looking with age. It's the same with people. The sign of time passing and expression lines show

character. Old people should be full members of our society, we can all benefit from their experience.' It's why older women such as Carmen Dell'Orefice and Polly Mellen appeared in his shows. 'I wasn't trying to be funny, but to make people see that you don't have to stay young-looking at any cost and have the "perfect" measurements to be beautiful and sexy and to wear my clothes.' Evelyn Tremois, then a 70-year-old grandmother in turquoise cashmere with a Hermès scarf, was a model he found at an open casting session at Galeries Lafayette. She told Georgina Howell in *Vogue* that she had heard that Gaultier was looking for mannequins between the ages of 70 and 77. 'Life has made me a little sad recently, I thought, why not?'

During the early Eighties, Gaultier admits he found the interchangeable classical physiques of towering Scandinavian models insipid. Instead of professionals striking artificial poses, he preferred real women who liked fashion and who didn't strut down the catwalk with the same robotic walk. He did not seek the blanket perfection of other designers, and his atypical muses included Farida Khelfa, a model of Algerian origins – 'I was so intimidated by her beauty, I had never seen anything as exotic as her before,' Gaultier recalls – along with Edwige Belmore, Queen of the Punks, Frédérique Lorca and Aitize Hanson, a model from Guadeloupe who was eventually to manage the Gaultier archives.

He has also hired forceful personalities such as the actresses Rossy de Palma and Valérie Lemercier, and full-figured models such

'I love and admire everyone who is different.'

JEAN PAUL GAULTIER

as Velvet D'Amour, Crystal Renn and Beth Ditto. One of his most enduring working relationships was with Anna Pawlowski. Gaultier recalls that she turned up one day at Jean Patou's *maison*. He told *Vogue*, 'She was like a Modigliani drawing come to life and with her bobbed hair cut into a Louise Brooks twenties style fringe, she was strikingly different from other models and would pad around Paris barefoot and in dresses from the 1940s.'

He frequently interspersed mannequins with real women of all shapes and sizes because he felt they understood and enjoyed clothes in a way an 'Amazonian', professional model was rarely capable of. He supplemented model-agency selections with open casting calls, recruiting with classified ads which read 'Non-conformist designer seeks unusual models – the conventionally pretty need not apply.' He railed against the fact that when working for other houses he could not use black models because, as the *rendeuses* at Jean Patou had once explained to him, 'the American clients might not like it', and he swore to 'trample all over those barriers' when he began his first ready-to-wear collection.

Beth Ditto in Gaultier's frothy concoction of tulle bodice and fishnet tights for the spring/ summer 2011 ready-to-wear collection. Ditto was one of several larger women whom Gaultier hired to model his clothes. He found that using 'unusual models' could have a powerful impact.

Overleaf Model Sophie Dahl wears a long ivory satin corset dress with matching long gloves for Gaultier's 2001 spring/summer couture collection. Dahl's fuller – and more normal – figure, like Gaultier's 'anything goes' casting sessions, challenged fashion's conventional ideals of what was beautiful.

The model and designer Inès de La Fressange recalled that very early on in his career every model wanted to work with him because of the person he was – his warm personality – and because of his work as a designer. Well-known and in-demand models were not given preferential treatment: Carla Bruni, the musician, model and former First Lady of France, remembers turning up for one of his public casting shows.

'Everybody was always welcome on his catwalk whatever age, body shape, skin colour, gender.'

THIERRY-MAXIME LORIOT, CURATOR

'A MILITANT ICONOCLAST, HE SYSTEMATICALLY QUESTIONS STEROTYPES, STANDARDS, CODES CONVENTIONS AND TRADITIONS.'

NATHALIE BONDIL, ART CURATOR

'I showed up one day at a casting session because he was the only designer I hadn't yet done any runway work for. I was already known as a model, but I undoubtedly had too classic a look for him. I waited two hours like everyone else to show him my books.'

It didn't always go to plan; the buxom Velvet D'Amour elicited much mirth in the audience when she modelled the *Sporty Chic* collection in 2006, something that Gaultier had never intended. His purpose he told *Vogue* was never to disguise or ridicule. 'Maybe it's the fashion superman side of me, who wants to make people see beauty where seemingly there is none. If people believe I want to make them laugh, then I've failed to make my point because that's not my intention.'

In tune with the the social, creative and sexual pulse of the moment, Gaultier's strength has always been his experience and knowledge of a world outside the confines of Paris fashion, along with cultural interests that are considerably broader than those of many French fashion designers. In the mid-Seventies, Gaultier understood that fashion was undergoing seismic change and that the rarefied domain of haute couture was out of touch with what else was happening in the world. He began to understand that the vibrancy of fashion ultimately lay with ready-to-wear. He realised very early on (like Yves Saint Laurent, a design hero of his, had done) that clothes were only part of fashion and that true fashion belonged to a cultural movement which needed to take into account all aspects of society, namely what people wore on the street, the music they listened to, the restaurants they frequented. As he told *Women's Wear Daily* in 1984, 'Everything that passes before my eyes is turned into a fashion reflex. My passions are hugely visual.'

London beckoned and offered him a rich vein of inspiration. As Colin McDowell observes, 'the popstars who really excited him were British and he responded well to the androgynous appeal of David Bowie and the sexual omnivore that was Mick Jagger'.

Farida Khelfa wearing a black taffeta fishtail dress and embellished jacket on the catwalk for Gaultier's 2011 Punk Cancan collection. His atypical muses included Khelfa, a model of Algerian origins.

Overleaf Two photographs by Herb Ritts capture the sensual and erotic charge of Gaultier's designs. A sultry-looking Tatjana Patitz (left) in mesh body stocking and black diamond-patterned tabard references Gaultier's love of punk. His kaleidoscopic knowledge of fashion took in everything from the haute couture world in the 1960s to the current street scene in Pigalle, which inspired this dramatic boned, strapless viscose jersey dress in black (right).

He regularly visited the capital, often accompanying his friend Aitize Hanson when she went there to model, and he would go to hear Siouxsie and the Banshees, Soft Cell, The Clash and the Sex Pistols. The punk phenomenon influenced him a lot. Even given his happy, comfortable and loving childhood, he felt the need to rebel – to rebel against the conformism of a petty-minded bourgeois Paris filled with its restricting rules.

Hanson remembers how they had gone together to see *The Rocky Horror Picture Show* in Chelsea. 'He loved the androgynous, rocker-style outfits in the film. He also really liked the way English people dressed. We often went to London for the weekend, to Portobello Road to see the shops and the second-hand clothing stores. Because of his incredible memory, he was like a recording machine out on the streets – he picked up on everything, deciphering how people put their looks together, the colours, the fabrics, the details of the clothes.' As Gaultier told *Vogue*, he took pleasure in seeing grown men in bowler hats alongside their sons with Mohawk haircuts; and the punks' fishnet stockings, tribal make-up, bondage straps, kilts and rubber trousers were to inspire his future collections.

B ack in Paris after his stint working in the Philippines for Pierre Cardin he was determined to use all the experiences of the last few years to create a true place for himself in French fashion. By chance, he met his oldest friend at school, Donald Potard, who introduced him to Francis Menuge, a man who, while not explicitly involved in fashion, was interested in creating modern, electronic jewellery. Menuge was to become Gaultier's business partner and the man who Gaultier would describe as the love of his life.

'Even though I like the fashions of the past and am constantly looking to the future, my main influence is what's happening today.'

JEAN PAUL GAULTIER

Encouraged by Potard and Menuge, he was persuaded into showing his first ready-to-wear collection in 1976. It wasn't easy, and he was faced with a problem: 'In France you can't just go and set up a stall as you might in Portobello market. There's a process here. You need a backer before people will take you seriously,' he explained to *Vogue*. With the help of his family and his friends (his cousin knitted the sweaters, the concierge of his apartment building helped make the clothes, the chief hairdresser at the Alexandre de Paris salon did the hair and Menuge made the accessories) and using his own money, Gaultier presented his first collection in 1976 at the Palais de la Découverte. While Menuge handled the business arrangements, everything was done on a shoestring and no one was paid.

Agyness Deyn appears in Gaultier's 30th anniversary catwalk retrospective during the spring/summer 2007 shows. The leather jacket, studded bodice and taffeta skirt is an outfit from his first collection, shown in 1976.

There was a mix-up with the timing and any fashion journalist of note had gone to Emmanuelle Khanh's show. 'The ones who had come to me were ancient and had come expecting drinks but we had nothing to give them,' Gaultier laughs. Still, the room was full, even if most of the audience were gate-crashers. There were nine models, who wore dresses made from fabrics bought from the Marché Saint Pierre, jackets made from cross-stitch or raffia placemats, piped canvas, upholstery *toile de Jouy*; and biker jackets worn over ballet tutu skirts with trainers, together with the first electronic jewellery made by Menuge. 'It was,' Gaultier recalls, 'a muddle of a collection' but the clothes were sexy and witty, making use of a mishmash of materials in an interesting, unlikely way.

There were only nine journalists at Gaultier's first show, but the collection nevertheless gained attention, particularly at first from the Japanese and British press. Martin Margiela, who went on to be Gaultier's most high-profile assistant, remembers that first collection. 'I didn't have an invitation but, with all the confusion caused by the crowd, I was able to attend the show of a new designer on the scene: Jean Paul Gaultier. There was a really fun atmosphere before it began, but you saw more tough guys than major editors in the hall. I was seized by an excitement I had never felt before. Then – and it was a

total surprise – I saw girls from Les Halles [in the 1970s an edgy, hip area where girls who liked fashion would gravitate] and fashionable clubs come out among the models. Together, they embodied Jean Paul's vision of a very laid-back Parisienne.'

Lucinda Chambers, *Vogue*'s Fashion Director, remembers her first Gaultier show as if it was yesterday. 'It was one where the models wore body suits as if tattooed from head to toe. I was in shock ... but of wonder and amazement. I hadn't seen a show that could carry you away, that it was not about clothes, it was about being in someone else's head, they were characters, men and women, all different shapes and sizes. But all in this wonderful fantasy that was so beautiful and transporting and yet using references that we see every day. It felt very French. It was so polished and complete.'

Not that it was easy at the start; Gaultier financed those early collections by working for Chombert Furs and the Indian importer Mayagor. He also managed to sell some designs to Victoire which was 'the' boutique at the time. He used a few of his designs for Mayagor and some of his furs for Chombert to fill out his second collection, which was loosely based on Robin Hood. According to Colin McDowell, the show 'had its moments of theatre of the absurd, not least when, in the dark, nobody could find the shoes for the models and they had to go out without them.'

It wasn't really until his fourth collection that people began to seriously talk about the new boy on the scene. Then the journalist Melka Tréanton introduced him to Dominique Emschwiller, who was instrumental in bringing him together with the Japanese Kashiyama Group, and his clothes were then sold at Emschwiller's influential Paris boutique, Bus Stop. Georgina Howell reported in American *Vogue* that 'the turning point came in 1978 when Kashiyama began to finance his operations and he could have a real studio, with a design assistant, pattern-maker and seamstress. They backed him for the Sixties-inspired and very well received *James Bond* collection in 1979 that finally made his name.' The funding also enabled Gaultier to advertise, which played a key role in getting the label recognised. In 1981, Gaultier started manufacturing with the Italian company Gibo, while Kashiyama continued to produce under licence for Japan and the Far East.

From the early 1980s, Gaultier began introducing a diversity of genres and a wide range of looks. And, he was sending a powerful message: be yourself, no matter what nature and education have dealt you. He had found his method of mix and match, collect, convert and combine. His approach represented the convergence of traditions: those of the ateliers of haute couture and of the street. He would mix genres and recycle past epochs with dizzying virtuosity, like a Surrealist collagist. He would cut and paste, matching up precisely those things which did not match. He told *Vogue* that he 'liked things which were tacky, people who dressed badly. The people who dress badly, who make mistakes, are the ones who interest me,' and yet he was proud to have trained in the fundamentals of haute couture, to know the secret of elegance. Moreover, it was the technique and craftsmanship of Gaultier's collections in the early Eighties that gained him his place in the fashion establishment.

Gaultier admired the technique and craftsmanship of Rei Kawakubo, Gianni Versace, Azzedine Alaïa, Giorgio Armani and Thierry Mugler, and their work, too, although it was often very different from his own. Of Mugler he admitted that he had tried to do the opposite of what he was doing. 'He was very creative, his shows were very creative, always full-scale spectacles: opera, actresses, superstars, the glamorous sashay … but that wasn't my thing.' Not that Gaultier's shows were by any means low key. They fizzed

Still modelling in her eighties, Carmen Dell'Orefice appears in Gaultier's autumn/winter 2014 Rosbifs in Space wearing a silver lamé trench coat over a silver sequin jumpsuit. Gaultier believed that women didn't have to stay young-looking at any cost or have the 'perfect' measurements in order to look good wearing his clothes.

'I always wanted to design collections to suit women of different styles and all ages.'

JEAN PAUL GAULTIER

with energy and as Carine Roitfeld recounts, his 'presentations were as eagerly anticipated as the shows of rockstars. There are incredible crowds and, every season the fashion editors argue over who gets a seat.' John Duka in American *Vogue* wrote of how they were staged in the most unusual of venues: from the Cirque d'Hiver, a nineteenth-century amphitheatre in Paris, to the Grande halle de la Villette in the Parc de la Villette, an enormous glass and cast-iron space where he once displayed one hundred outfits on one hundred models appearing on a conveyor belt.

By the end of the Seventies as many as 4000 people were lining up to see his collections. On the 31st March, 1980 *Women's Wear Daily* reported that his clothes reflected what was going on in youth culture. No longer a fringe attraction, he was finally a serious success. As fashion commentators like McDowell have pointed out, there is a powerful link between advertising revenue and editorial coverage. With costly shows and advertising campaigns bolstering Gaultier's name he soon became a fashion personality, a designer whose views were solicited by radio and TV chat shows. It wasn't just his designs (eccentric even by the standards of some of the wackier Eighties' creations) but his attitudes which delighted and dismayed the fashion world in equal measure. 'Many' notes McDowell 'were impressed by his sharp intelligence and verbal fluency. It didn't hurt either that he had a kaleidoscopic fashion knowledge, from haute couture in the Sixties to the current street scene of Pigalle and was able to speak of it as fluently in English as he was in French.'

Gilded majesty (left) – an ornate opera-style coat with fur trim collar and gold embellishment, and embroidery that nods to the Vienna Secession art movement; the surprise factor of tartan beneath Gaultier's unzipped skirt (middle) adds interest to a long dress which is worn with a red furry jacket; both photographed by Michel Arnaud. The swoosh of a floor-skimming gown in salmon pink – Gaultier's signature colour – (right) on a model whose hairstyle demonstrates Gaultier's predilection for non-conformist hair and make-up. Photograph by Roger Dean.

'The shock of the way I mix patterns and fabrics can be disconcerting, but what I am trying to do is provoke new ideas about how pieces can be put together in different ways.'

JEAN PAUL GAULTIER

In 1983 Gaultier presented the *Dada* collection, one that to this day remains dear to him because it is when he first showed the idea of corset-style dresses and jumpsuits. In that year, too he presented his first men's ready-to-wear collection. By this time he was established. *Women's Wear Daily* gave him a front page headline declaring him Paris's court jester who had entered the court of Paris Titans with a wit-filled packed collection. *The Face* was even more flattering, proclaiming him the true star of Paris fashion week.

He designed Junior Gaultier in 1988 not for the sake of selling clothes or making money, according to John Duka in American *Vogue*, but because he found himself in an embarrassing position: the young loved his clothes but couldn't afford them. So Gaultier did the obvious thing: he created a collection specifically for them which ranged in price from 250–500 French Francs. More than 450,000 garments were sold in a single season at his Paris boutique on the rue du Jour.

The first Jean Paul Gaultier boutique had opened in the Galerie Vivienne in 1985. He had closed a side street off the Place des Victoires where he staged a street-scene carnival that included jugglers, mime artists and plenty of candyfloss. It was a fitting scene given his predilection for circus-style catwalk antics. His unique ability to mix materials, question the canons of good taste and make exciting juxtapositions of ethnic elements and traditional Parisian chic made it clear to fashion watchers that an original new talent was emerging. And this was only the beginning.

This show-stopping green sequin suit displays many signature Gaultier themes – sensuality, the blurring of the masculine and feminine, immaculate tailoring and a determination to dazzle and entertain. In this 1990 cover image for Vogue Paris, *photographer and Gaultier collaborator Jean-Baptiste Mondino captures the designer's zest for life.*

'The Eighties and the Nineties were really his years. When we were going to Paris, Jean Paul Gaultier was the one you went to see.'

FRANCA SOZZANI, VOGUE ITALIA

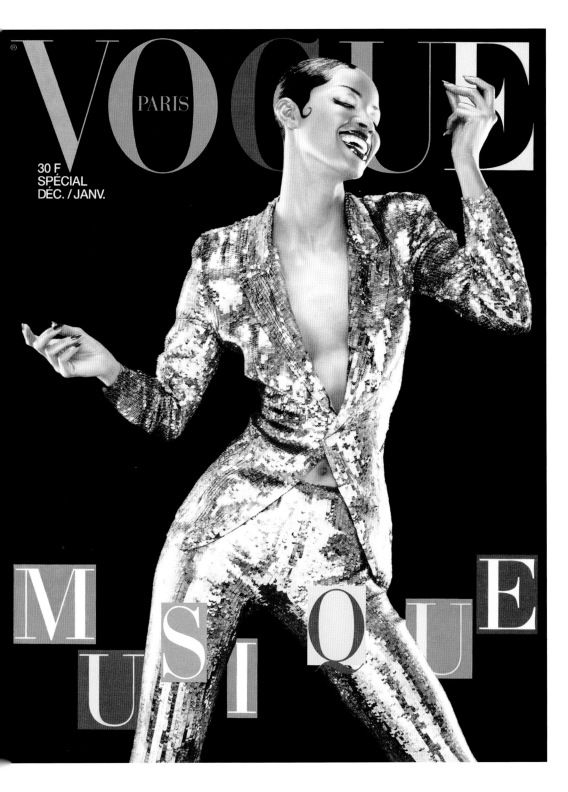

'HE TINKERS, SALVAGES, REARRANGES,
JUXTAPOSES, BUILDING UPON
CONTRASTS AND CONTRADICTIONS TO
INVENT AN AESTHETIC OF PARADOX,
AMBIGUITY THAT IS HIS ALONE.'

NATHALIE BONDIL, ART CURATOR

GLOBAL NOMAD IN PARIS AND LONDON

Gaultier's fascination with Indian jewellery was awakened when, working for Pierre Cardin in 1974, he stopped off in India and Nepal en route to the Philippines. This began a lifelong appreciation of ethnic design and decoration. From the beginning, Gaultier was also enormously inspired by the rich tapestry of street fashion in London and Paris, and when it came to designing his clothes, he constantly sought to elevate the everyday and integrate the bizarre. About his *Around the World in 168 Outfits* collection in 1988 he told John Duka in *Vogue*, 'It's Calcutta, not New Delhi. It's Oriental but in an Occidental way, so people won't look at it and say, "Ha! India!" It's extreme body shapes, it's playing with things that are almost bad taste.'

As *Vogue* reported, Gaultier based entire collections on the attire of Hasidic Jews or the sealskins of Inuits. He put everything into the twentieth-century blender (music hall, 1940s' elegance, cinema, punk) whizzing it all together for comic and witty effect, producing kimonos which were spliced onto a double-breasted suit or trench coats that were also dresses, and always a joy to behold. In the introduction to *The Fashion World of Jean Paul Gaultier: From the Sidewalk to the Catwalk*, the volume that accompanied the exhibition celebrating his 35 years in fashion, art curator Nathalie Bondil describes Gaultier's vision as postmodern: 'He tinkers, salvages, rearranges, juxtaposes, building upon contrasts and contradictions to invent an aesthetic of paradox, ambiguity that is his alone.'

As Gaultier told *Madame Figaro*, his former head of Couture, Catherine Lardeur, had once described him as a 'bit bi-polar: eccentric but also very classic.' Gaultier answered this charge by saying, 'Not just a bit! … I like to make bi-polar dresses: I've always loved the idea of morphing, passing from one mood to another, from masculine to feminine.' Much in the way that he loved to promote different standards of beauty, Gaultier's imagination was taken with multi-cultural, multi-gender influences.

This Pamela Hanson image shows how Gaultier delights in Eastern influences. The cheongsam is reworked for a Western audience in a burgundy velvet tunic with pale blue trim worn with a headdress of exotic silk flowers.

Overleaf *Vogue said of Gaultier's design (left): 'Minimalism might reign elsewhere but here, the exotic and the delicate and the rich make dressing an exercise in artistry.' Stella Tennant wears a Nehru collar lilac silk jacket over a bodice with mother-of-pearl buttons and cream tulle long dress. Photograph by Paolo Roversi. Gaultier wittily mixes Western and Eastern influences (right). David Sims photographs a heavily embellished velvet devoré coat teamed with wide-leg trousers and Japanese sandals.*

Years before 'LBGT' issues were the fashionable choices for newspaper op-ed columns, he was happy to promote fusion fashion. And while other designers in the late Seventies or early Eighties played with opulence or a fantasy world of extravagance and wealth, Gaultier was far more interested in referencing the street. He drew inspiration from punks from across the Channel adorned in tattoos, leather and metal spikes, and also from the culturally rich, multi-ethnic neighbourhoods of Paris where he was moved by African women who wore men's overcoats over vibrantly coloured traditional dress.

'Everything I've ever designed,' Gaultier told *Vogue*, 'has always been done in a context.' And while the fashion of the past inspires him, he is aroused by everything that surrounds him in the present. In another interview with the magazine he said that, 'Fashion must correspond to the aspirations of the moment and reflect current events. To do that, designers must have their antennas out and pick up on, observe, listen to and think about everything.' He does precisely that.

Gaultier has long been influenced by the colours, fabrics and embellishments of traditional Indian dress and has embraced them in his designs. Here a model wears a turban and embroidered aproned tunic top and wide trousers from his spring/summer 2000 couture collection entitled, Les Indes Galantes.

Overleaf Indian style at Gaultier. The designer told Vogue: 'It was all about elegant slumming [including] a tiered chiffon dress with a sari slant.' Photographed by Andrew Lamb.

There were frequent trips to London to absorb all he could, a city in which he felt liberated and which lacked the small-minded, bourgeois attitudes to dress and social mores that he has consequently spent the rest of his life rebelling against. He felt that Parisians were shackled by the preconceived diktats of supposed 'good taste'. As he told Caroline Kellett in *Vogue*, 'London is brimming with young, unconventional glamour. I never fail to be inspired by it. I translate some of this rawness and eccentricity into my own collections; I also draw ideas from music, old films, new videos, anything that distils the essence of youth and style. As a designer I believe one can no longer create from the ivory tower of the couturier.

'How can we tweak the sexual, aesthetic, ethnic and religious codes that determine social conventions?

JEAN PAUL GAULTIER

'ALWAYS MY COLLECTIONS ARE MADE OF DIFFERENT INFLUENCES.'

JEAN PAUL GAULTIER

One must combine and enjoy many disciplines – that is why I admire Malcom McLaren [the designer, impresario and manager of the Sex Pistols] so much and the multi-talented scene he is involved in. One day I intend to open a shop catering for an entire lifestyle: my clothes for men and women plus all the paraphernalia – records, books, furniture – that would go with them.' What Gaultier so admired in London was the particular humour that he didn't find elsewhere, particularly when it came to dressing. 'You're so good at making fun of yourself here,' he told *Vogue*, 'Whereas in France people feel that they always have to be serious, tasteful, and adhere to these very specific ways of dressing.'

I n a radical move, Gaultier brought racial diversity to the catwalk with his legendary *Barbès* show in 1984. The title referenced an area of Paris that was far removed from couture's historic centre, and which he opened up to the fashion press, where Algerian and Senegalese immigrants had created a world of their own. 'It was a collection inspired by an ethnic ratatouille of North African, Caribbean and Oriental cultures in the immigrant 18th arrondissement' reported Georgina Howell in American *Vogue*. 'Why not?' Gaultier asked her, of the possibility of mixing cultures. 'We all wear American jeans, buy Chinese take-out.' Aitize Hanson remembers that it was a very colourful collection and the perfect embodiment of the idea of mixing up people, gender and diversity. It was designed for the streets and to be chic and wearable all at the same time. 'The idea was quite complicated' Gaultier told *Vogue*, 'as I wanted to present this idea of a multi-layered identity: there were African women who live in France but continue their traditions because they don't want to erase their culture but they also assimilate a new culture, so I mixed this dandy look with a traditional African attire. The models had to wear around four layers which they gradually peeled off … so you can imagine how long it took to get everyone dressed. I don't think we slept for three nights.'

Peter Lindbergh photographs Gaultier's iconic strapless dress in orange velvet, which introduced his exaggerated conical breast shapes. The dress is from the designer's celebrated Barbès *collection.*

Overleaf *Patrick Demarchelier captures Gaultier's global nomad spirit (left), inspired by a myriad cultures and countries, with a dramatic gypsy skirt teamed with a crepon blouse and sash belt. A yellow silk halterneck gown from Gaultier Paris, the couture collection (right). It has the daring, exuberance and drama of clothes from South America, combined with a mastery of tailoring workmanship. The blue feathered headpiece adds a touch of the exotic. Photograph by Mario Testino.*

The power of Gaultier's shows has always been not just in the exquisite clothes themselves, the drama of their presentation and original choice of music, but in the statements that they have made – light-hearted or deep – about society. Another collection that reflected the cultural melting pot was his *Le Retour de l'imprimé* (*Return of the Print*) collection for spring/summer 1984 which was a mixture of African and European dress, making boubous – the wide-sleeved robes worn by men in much of West Africa – out of draped tunics, and with miniskirts covering his models' heads. Later, he reworked Chinese tunics and brocade satin trousers, Japanese kimonos and Romanian peasant blouses for *Le Grand Voyage*, autumn/winter 1994, which drew inspiration from Mongolia, Tibet, China and Inuit culture, and for which he dressed up Linda Evangelista in a Mongolian outfit. Fashion editor Suzy Menkes described his *Les Tatouages* (*Tattoos*) collection for spring/summer 1994 as a celebration of body decoration, 'particularly, the magnificent meld of pierced noses and primitive tattoos on body stocking tops. The multi-ethnic clothes included Tuareg costumes, Moroccan braiding, Nehru jackets, eighteenth-century frockcoats and crinolines created from patches of denim jeans.'

A shot by Jean Marc Manson for Vogue's feature 'A day in the life of Linda Evangelista' shows the supermodel in a Mongolian-inspired outfit from Gaultier's autumn/ winter 1994 Le Grand Voyage *collection, which also referenced Tibetan, Chinese and Inuit culture.*

In 1997, Gaultier decided to dedicate his autumn/winter prêt-à-porter show to black culture, as a tribute to the singers Miriam Makeba and Nina Simone. It was to be shown on 24 black models and one white one. Around the same time the French government had started to limit immigration so, by the time the show came around, what had been intended as an aesthetic decision had become a political one. 'My most abiding memory of Gaultier's shows,' says fashion editor Laura Craik, is that 'season after season, he showcased true diversity – of the sort that paved the way for, say Olivier Rousteing, as I'm sure he would be the first to admit. Not just diversity of race – no single tokenistic black model – but diversity of race, age, gender and spirit.'

Gaultier's most impressive statement in his early shows was his vision of diversity across Europe and especially France. Referring

to previous immigrants, the Russian aristocrats in the 1920s, he underlines the differences between those cultivated and elitist arrivals and the post-war workers. Gaultier told Suzy Menkes, 'We are now at the second, third and fourth generations of immigrants who have been absorbed.' A 1997 collection entitled *Russia* caught the moment when a resurgent, post-Communist Russia was about to send big luxury spenders to the West, and when a wave of Eastern European migrants were set to arrive. Menkes remembers the surrealism of this haute couture show, with the extraordinary top-hat-shaped head pieces that were actually sculpted from hair. And how the legendary hairdresser Alexandre de Paris told her the braids were used to express a romantic Eastern European mood which took three months for his studio to create.

Russia had already featured in the early *Constructivist* (or *Russian*) collection, which was more about hybrid materials. Cyrillic lettering heightened the clash of leather, vinyl, sequins and jersey. This was a visually powerful show staged in the Grande Halle de la Villette in 1986 with the models appearing on a metallic grid.

Further global inspiration was revealed in the tribute to the artist Frida Kahlo for spring/summer 1998; sacks of tropical fruit and coffee beans spilled over a runway with a backdrop of banana leaves, the sweetness tempered by the smoke of Cuban cigars and an air of Che Guevara machismo. It exemplified the elegance of Latin America, showing the influence of dress styles from Mexico, Brazil, Argentina and Cuba.

An exotic floral headdress with a diagonally cut patterned top, shawl and wide-leg trousers, from Gaultier's homage to Frida Kahlo in his 1998 spring/ summer ready-to-wear collection. Photograph by Andrew Lamb.

Overleaf A model wears Gaultier's stretch tulle t-shirt with accessories including beads and a nose chain, all from the collection, Les Tatouages, spring/summer 1994, which sought inspiration from Africa and the Pacific Islands and was a celebration of body decoration. Photograph by Frederik Lieberath.

'Everything I've ever designed
has always been done in a context'.

JEAN PAUL GAULTIER

'PUNK OR
STREET FASHION
OR A TATTOO-
COVERED
BODY, THAT IS
INTERESTING
TO ME, AND
THAT I LOVE.'

JEAN PAUL GAULTIER

But as Menkes points out, Gaultier is more than a maker of sets and purveyor of dreams. Shock and discomfort greeted the *Chic Rabbis* collection for autumn/winter 1994 from the moment that music from *Fiddler on the Roof* was played by a lone violinist and the models proceeded down the gallery lit with menorahs. Their curled side-locks, flat, furry hats and long narrow coats – not to mention Gaultier's skull cap matching his striped sweater – left no doubt that this was a fashion take on Orthodox, particularly Hasidic, Judaism. As Gaultier has explained since, he was in a taxi in New York when he passed the New York Public Library, and at that moment a group of 150 rabbis descended the steps like a flock of birds. 'I was fascinated. I found them very beautiful, very elegant with their hats and their huge coats flapping in the wind. It was a fantastic scene, although I was afraid [the resulting collection] would be poorly received. But the fashion press were generally enthusiastic. Anna Wintour really liked it.' Photographers such as Steven Meisel, Ellen Von Unwerth and Steven Klein photographed the top models of the day with pieces from the collection. Kurt Cobain wore some of the pieces in his music videos.

If anyone found it disappointing, it was not for political reasons but because many, according to *Vogue*, more accustomed to Gaultier's visual exuberance, found it underwhelming. Not among them was Carine Roitfeld, who was also responsible for shooting two of his ad campaigns in the mid-Nineties. She recalls that it was a 'huge challenge, to pay tribute to traditional Jewish dress, but Jean Paul met it brilliantly by designing an outstanding collection and show. More than a fashion designer, he is, along with John Galliano, the best stylist I know. He knows how to put clothes together.'

Religion was also explored in the collection *Rap'pieuses* – (*Rap'sisters* or *Rap'prayers*). Gaultier says he had been keen to pay homage to religion without focusing on any one in particular. The models came up through the floor on turntables dressed as nuns.

Gaultier's 1993 Chic Rabbis *collection was inspired by Hasidic dress and culture. The designer said he loved the elegance of the hats and huge coats, but though many fashion writers were supportive, the collection was criticised for cultural insensitivity. Photograph by Andrew Lamb.*

Overleaf A bohemian and feminine swirling paisley chiffon slip dress (left) with ruched, patterned leggings and a silk print, layered peignoir. Photograph by Javier Vallhonrat. This floor-swooshing maxi dress (right), here teamed with colourful bangles, its bold patterns and fringed hem refences the clothing of Latin America. Photograph by Lee Broomfield.

'The 1989 show of *Rap'sisters* was one of my favourite Gaultier shows,' says fashion editor Lisa Armstrong. 'It seemed quite daring and naughty at the time but the clothes were fabulous. There was always so much that was wearable and classic.'

For his *Bad Girls–Point G* (*G-spot*) collection for spring/summer 2010, Gaultier spelled out and amplified the message of community he had begun with the *Barbès* collection. The invitation to the show resembled the map of France found in schools in the 1950s, but the departments had been replaced with the outlines of Morocco, Togo, Russia, Mexico and Greece. The message was clear: France's identity is fed by sources beyond its borders. Burnouses, harem pants, Mongolian jackets, Swedish socks, Chinese dresses, Masai necklaces, turbans and babouche (pointed, Turkish-style) slippers mixed with Gaultier wardrobe classics including the trench coat and the corset. These different wardrobe staples were a symbolic illustration of how much the intermingling of peoples enriches a country's cultural and artistic heritage.

Gaultier constantly reworked his signature corset shape throughout his 40-year career. In the dress (left) from his 2010 Bad Girls–Point G collection, photographed by Jason Lloyd-Evans, he uses contrast to emphasise, as he so often did, the shape of the breasts. A corset dress (right) from the 1990 Les Rap'pieuses collection, photographed by Michel Arnaud, has contrast contour panelling, giving the outfit a graphic silhouette.

Of course, in embracing cultural diversity and striving to reflect society and the changing times, Gaultier was also well versed in reflecting changes in the role of women and their place in the world of work in the Eighties. One of his earliest influences was the Sixties designer André Courrèges. Gaultier once saw him on the television, and he was struck by the way he talked about the women who wore his designs. Instead of talking about clothes, the way other designers might, Courrèges talked about real women, who were active, who drove their own cars, who worked, who ran – real live women. 'I thought "My God, that's incredible." It was about human beings, and extremely modern,' Gaultier said. And so it made him think about designing for women as they are – as fully rounded human beings rather than some impossible paradigm or object. He told *Vogue*, 'Women have traumatised themselves for the past twenty years, often spoiled their health and frazzled their nerves for a physical ideal.'

Roars of applause greeted his first men's collection in spring/ summer 1984 with its exotic exposure of the back of the body and the title *L'Homme-Objet* (*Man as Object* or *Boy Toy*) – just at the time when women in the workplace were donning power suits with big-shouldered jackets, complaining about being treated as sex objects but still worrying about the need to look attractive.

As he realised, the Eighties was the decade when every woman did a job and defined themselves though their work rather than their relationships. And yet even if they did need to show that they had a head for business, there was a pressure to look as if they still had 'a body for sin'. As Georgina Howell in *Vogue* observed, 'As fashion always reflects the times, the central sort of women's fashion this decade has been the split between work and the rest of life, between office and bedroom, authority and approachability. Martians would puzzle over this decade's paradox of increasing womanpower and the riot of sexy and frivolous fashion.'

Gaultier's first men's collection in 1984, with its man-as-object theme, delighted observers. Here Gaultier indulges his sense of humour by showing us what every man needs in his wardrobe: an outfit entirely made from Aran knit wool. Photograph by Michel Arnaud.

Gaultier has always preferred the company of women to that of men. He told *Vogue* that he believed that women are quite frankly more intelligent than men, perhaps because they 'have to think more in order to get what they want, because the world is run by machos'. Many commentators feel that Gaultier set out to empower women. 'He coaxed us into tailoring that was strong and sexy and which had all the power codes normally reserved for men's clothes,' said Lisa Armstrong. 'His tailoring was a million miles from the fussy, pussy-bow blouse and puff-sleeved jackets that formed the basis of early 80s female "power" dressing. There was always a sense of humour to his shows which made the clothes seem extra chic.'

'FROM PUTTING MEN IN SKIRTS TO
MAKING UNDERWEAR OUTERWEAR,
HE HAS BEEN MORE DARING, AND
CONSIDERABLY MORE RADICAL,
THAN ANY OTHER DESIGNER.'

VALERIE STEELE, FASHION HISTORIAN

THE GENDER BLENDER

There are two items of clothing that will stand out as milestones in Jean Paul Gaultier's work: the reinvented corset and the skirt he designed for men. The conical bra basque corset worn by Madonna on her Blond Ambition World Tour in 1990, particularly in the picture of the star onstage with her pony-tail swish of platinum blonde, is unforgettable. The corsets Gaultier designed now rank alongside Marilyn Monroe's white halter-neck dress and Audrey Hepburn's Givenchy little black dress in fashion iconography. In many ways, Gaultier's corseted women seemed like the negation of the feminist struggles of the 1960s and 1970s, especially as fashion was embracing a new group of designers which included the Yohji Yamamoto and Rei Kawakubo, whose clean-lined and geometric clothing was austere rather than overtly feminine. But in reality Gaultier prompted another kind of female emancipation.

No union could have been better than Gaultier's collaboration with Madonna. It spoke of his love affair with pop stars and pop music but also of his desire for strong, individual, idiosyncratic women. As Suzy Menkes writes: 'The burgeoning sexual freedom of women, seeded in the 1960s, culminated in Gaultier's costume designs for Madonna's 1990 Blond Ambition World Tour. This rebel with a corset moment was when runway and stage merged, bringing to a global public the vision of the conical bra that the designer had revealed first on the catwalk in 1983 with his Dada collection.'

By the mid Eighties, Gaultier had collaborated with a number of artists. He had designed costumes for the French actress Annie Girardot, and for dance performances choreographed by Régine Chopinot, but he had never worked with a star as famous as Madonna, who asked him to design costumes for her tour. There were 358 in total and it took eight people a good four months, including weekends, to sew the 150 kilos of stage costumes. *Madame Figaro* later revealed that in the run-up to her tour, Madonna lost weight after her final fitting, which meant that all her costumes had to be remade.

Madonna wears Gaultier's gold conical bra corset on her 1990 Blond Ambition World Tour. This image exemplifies one of the most iconic collaborations between the fashion and music worlds.

Overleaf *A men's black skirt, worn with matching jacket and trousers (left). Gaultier's men's skirts had their antecedents in sarongs, kilts and aprons. Photograph by Chris Moore. Gaultier's 1940s-inspired pale pink corset worn with a military-style strong-shouldered skirt suit (right). Photograph by Jason Lloyd-Evans.*

VOGUE

FEB
£2·20

THE NEW

MADONNA

THE NEW
COLLECTIONS
BOLD
BRIGHT
BEAUTIFUL

W hile the start of the Nineties was a career high for Gaultier, the death of Francis Menuge, his boyfriend and business partner who died of AIDS, was a tragedy. He admits that when Menuge died he thought he would 'give up' and told *Vogue Paris* that he questioned whether it was even worth continuing. 'It had been our story together.

Herb Ritts captures a brunette Madonna on the cover of Vogue *wearing Gaultier's romantic, Indian-inspired dress, projecting a gentler image than in her 'glamazon' corset, though breast shapes à la Gaultier are still defined, here by swirling spirals.*

This brand was like a child that we had together and I knew that I had to continue to bring it up'. The Madonna commission, for which it had been agreed that the central leitmotif would be the corset look, sent Gaultier's stock soaring even higher. The tour was a sold-out success around the world, and Gaultier's costumes were acclaimed, in particular the pink full-length corset with its exaggerated conical bra cups. At the time, most women wouldn't have touched corsets with a barge pole but as *Vogue* reported, within weeks the phrase 'underwear as outerwear' was on the lips of the fashionable and underwear has never looked back since.

It was Malcom McLaren who had first had an inkling of how the beautiful partnership between pop and clothes could be nurtured into multi-headed global business deals that would be of enormous benefit to both the music industry and the rag trade. Madonna too has repeatedly demonstrated a voracious and highly sophisticated appetite for designer fashion that helps her create headlines. While Gaultier was already a fan of Madonna's – 'I did not collaborate with her because I thought it would further my career,' he said, – he would have known that this partnership could only enhance his profile. Gaultier would have been very aware that three minutes on MTV would reach more people than a lifetime of catwalk shows.

'His is my absolute favourite show … long before he did my world tour. He is always playing with the idea of gender, giving it a theatrical, humorous twist.'

MADONNA

Despite the fact that women had – historically, fairly recently – unshackled themselves from corsets, Gaultier viewed them as something which symbolised strong femininity. He had, after all, grown up surrounded by strong women and did not subscribe to the myth of the weaker sex. The fashion historian Valerie Steele believes that Gaultier has been instrumental in transforming the way people perceive the corset: 'Traditionally it was viewed as an instrument of female oppression, the cause of ill health, even death. When Gaultier reintroduced the corset, his presentation of it – particularly in the case of Madonna, but even before – projected an image of sexually powerful women. Instead of signifying oppression, it seemed to become a sign of women's liberation, of women assuming power, sexual power included, over their bodies. Madonna on stage wearing Gaultier couture projected an image of female empowerment and sensuality, and that was enormously influential.'

Mario Testino shoots Kate Moss in a corset from Gaultier's 2013 couture collection. Said Vogue: *'The conical bra in nude satin is as "Gaultier" as Breton stripes. Why hide it? A sheer tulle skirt will do nicely.'*

Even Madonna had no idea how much impact that tour and its costumes would end up having on the cultural landscape, although she had always admired Gaultier. She told Georgina Howell in American *Vogue*, 'His is my absolute favourite show – always, always Gaultier, long before he did my world tour. He is always playing with the idea of gender, of what is masculine and feminine, giving it a theatrical, humorous twist; it was a kind of political statement.'

Gaultier had grown up with the presence of his grandmother's corsets. He was not the least bit interested in the garments' orthopaedic function: for him, they invoked something extraordinary, fascinating and mysterious. He especially loved the soft peachy pink colour that they usually came in. Even though by the late Sixties they had totally gone out of fashion, in the early Eighties he worked with a professional corset-maker and adapted them to work with all kinds of clothes – jumpsuits, long dresses, short dresses – and he began to look at underwear in general in a very different way.

'I have loved corsets since I was small.'

JEAN PAUL GAULTIER

As Susan Orlean recounted in *The New Yorker*, seeing one of his employees come to work wearing a Chanel jacket, unbuttoned, over nothing but a lacy bra, Gaultier was reminded of his grandmother walking around in her slip. He decided to design some clothes that expanded on a theme of lingerie. 'In some of the pieces, he exaggerated the cups of the bra, so that they looked like inverted ice-cream cones or an African fertility carving. He called the collection *Dada*, and it was an immediate sensation. The corset-dresses were analysed for their politics – was dressing a woman in a corset enslaving or empowering? – and for their shock value. Gaultier says that he was surprised at the commotion. "I didn't know there would be a reaction," he said. "I did it quite naturally!"'

He told *Vogue*, 'Women had long since stopped wearing those old-fashioned garments. But when I started designing, young women had begun to reassert their femininity. They were reinventing the idea of the female sex object who became strong and free enough to play with the rules. It was Madonna who came to perfectly embody this type of woman. A good example is the slip dress from my *Dada* collection in 1983, a bit of peek-a-boo fun. There's a good dose of hypocrisy behind this dress, because it gave the impression that the model didn't know her underwear was showing.

A pale pink corseted dress from Gaultier's 1983 Dada collection, in which he first showed the corsets which were to become a leitmotif of his work. Photograph by Chris Moore.

Overleaf *Terry Richardson captures Gaultier's sense of daring and showmanship in an outfit lavishly decorated with black jet beaded fishnet and black heron feathers at the neck and wrists (left). Gaultier's elegant black tuxedo jacket from his first haute couture collection in 1997 is boldly cut with strong shoulders and a deep V-neck front (right). A mannish trilby is softened with black lace. Photograph by Mario Testino.*

'Gaultier's imagination creates multicultural, multisexual fashion, hybrid references, gender transgressions, canons without cliches, a fluid place devoid of discrimination, a unique 'fusion fashion.'

NATHALIE BONDIL, ART CURATOR

In reality, I had noticed that some girls were wearing oversize pullovers and had the habit of pulling them, baring their shoulders. That gave me the idea for sweater dresses with plunging necklines that exposed the lingerie underneath, something that was considered a real no no up until then.'

As his friend and model Farida Khelfa remarked: 'He will leave a legacy that is both aesthetic and political. There is no boundary for him between masculinity and femininity. What interests him is the ambiguity of the sexes, the mixing of genders. In that way, a woman who wears a corset-look dress or a bra underneath a tuxedo style jacket, who dresses by undressing, moves out of a private sphere and asserts herself as a woman. Unlike other couturiers, he likes triumphant women with a hint of masculinity about them, and men who are at ease with their feminine side. Such non-conformity is very characteristic of his work.'

Amanda de Cadenet shoots the American actress Amanda Peet wearing a silver sequined body and wool trousers. Shine and sparkle are juxtaposed with Gaultier's love of strict masculine tailoring.

Overleaf *Nick Knight shows Kate Moss in Gaultier's black embroidered sheer blouse which leaves little to the imagination. A good example of Gaultier's love for 'a bit of peek-a-boo fun', and of which Vogue said: 'When mastered, sheer works wonders in the boardroom and the bedroom.'*

In American *Vogue* Georgina Howell reported that, towards the end of the Eighties, what interested the French underground most was the mixing of opposites, and she identified 'three wicked witches of Paris' at the forefront of this movement who 'cooked up enough sexual, social and cultural shocks to rearrange the world through the medium of the young.' They were Gaultier, Jean-Baptiste Mondino, the fashion photographer and music video director, and Jean-Paul Goude, the graphic designer, photographer and advertising film director. 'We've been playing around with the differences between man and woman, rich and poor, black and white – it's very democratic!' Mondino told *Vogue*. 'Meanwhile, Jean Paul was turning fashion into style, using music, video, sex-shop paraphernalia, movies and the technical stuff that sports firms like Nike were churning out.'

'He likes people who have a sense
of adventure with their clothes.'

DITA VON TEESE

'I THINK HE WILL BE REMEMBERED FOR HIS TRANSGRESSION OF ALL THE RULES CONCERNING TASTE.'

VALERIE STEELE, FASHION HISTORIAN

Gaultier was keen to break down what he saw as artificial barriers between menswear and womenswear. Blurring the lines between men's and women's clothing was amply demonstrated in his 1985 collection, *A Wardrobe for Two*, and has always been at the crux of many of Gaultier's outfits. As Roger Tredre and Brenda Polan write in *The Great Fashion Designers*, (of Gaultier) 'Why shouldn't men wear skirts? His introduction of men's skirts in 1985 and constant repetition of the theme was no gimmick but was based on a fundamental belief that clothes should not be gender specific. "Masculinity is not connected to the clothes you're wearing – it's in the mind," he said.'

Celebrating his spectacular 40-year career at the 2015 Vogue festival, Erin O'Connor – powerfully dressed in his masculine-looking waistcoat and trousers – reminisced about her first encounter with Gaultier. 'It was like meeting the Wizard of Oz. I was like Dorothy, I didn't want to go home.' Photograph by Pamela Hanson.

Gaultier's men's skirts and corsets had their antecedents in sarongs, kilts and aprons and in old military and cavalry corsets. He has said that he had no intention of making a statement or of being provocative; he was inspired by tradition – including the long aprons that waiters wear in brasseries – by togas and kilts, and by one of his male models, who had shown up for a fitting wearing a sarong, looking very masculine. During the *ancien régime*, for a man to show his legs was a sign of phallic power. His first men's skirts were constructed like a pair of trousers: with two legs cut fairly wide and a panel of fabric covering them in front.

'I don't believe that fabrics have a gender, any more than certain garments do. I've always presented skirts in a very masculine way, on very 'manly' models wearing thick socks and heavy boots. That might explain why heterosexual men have taken to it more than homosexual men; they didn't have to prove their masculinity. That said, I could never have anticipated the effect my men's skirt would have on fashion.'

'What is masculine and what is feminine anyway? ... I am only happy when there is no discrimination.'

JEAN PAUL GAULTIER

Gaultier sold three thousand of his skirts in 1985 and continued for many years to include them in his men's collections. He has denied that they were ever a gay statement, but instead were a reflection of the way men were changing and becoming less macho. Gaultier was always fiercely honest about his sexuality (unlike, for example, Yves Saint Laurent who was secretive, for fear it would affect his sales). In the November issue of *Vogue* in 1983 Gaultier told Caroline Kellett that he had decided to do an *Homme Objet* range for men which included straightforward but sexy clothes: 'I have noticed young men taking more care over their appearance recently; I think it's just as important for them to look sharp and seductive as it is for women so I'm promoting equality of sex appeal.'

He thought that fashion was still full of outdated conventions and clichés that no longer fitted the times. In an interview with Gaby Wood for the *Observer*, he talked about jackets. A tradition he continued with, because it served a functional purpose, was the slippery lining of body and sleeves, which makes a jacket easier to slip on. But the fact that women's and men's jackets button up and cross over in opposite directions is a convention that some, including Gaultier, think arose because men needed to reach their wallets easily, in order to pay, for example, for dinner, whereas women, of course, would not be expected to pay. So Gaultier told Wood that he decided to challenge what he considered a cliché by reversing the directions.

'I don't believe that fabrics
have a gender, any more than
certain garments do.'

JEAN PAUL GAULTIER

Herb Ritts shows Tatjana Patitz in Gaultier's exquisitely cut black satin playsuit, a sharply tailored tuxedo style at once masculine and yet also very feminine.

Overleaf *Longtime Gaultier muse Tanel Bedrossiantz (left) models a feathered skirt and black satin jacket from the 2011* Punk Cancan *couture collection. Dusan Reljin (right) photographs a skimpy patched top and laces criss-crossing bare legs – an outfit both revealing and genderless.*

Page 117 *In a tribute to Gaultier for* Vogue, *Bruce Weber shows the actress Vinessa Shaw in his 'flasher' mac with a diamanté and pearl collar and pockets, over a black bustier.*

Wood considers this attitude to be Gaultier's most significant and perhaps most misunderstood trait: he adored fashion's dying traditions, which he constantly looked to revive and update. But as for convention, and the narrow outlook it suggested, he sought to crush it. His avant-garde attempt to introduce haute couture for men was a financial failure, but his line of make-up for men was a success. The first men's cosmetic and skin line, 'Tout Beau, Tout Propre' was launched in 2003.

Fashion historian Valerie Steele sums up Gaultier's gender blending: 'I believe that his playing with the concepts of gender and sexuality will be regarded as one of the key aspects of his career. From putting men into skirts to making underwear outwear, he has been much more daring and considerably more radical than any other designer. Most importantly, I think he will be remembered for his transgression of all the rules concerning taste. With Gaultier, suddenly bad taste became as interesting, or at least as acceptable, as good taste, and better than no taste at all.'

'Jean Paul Gaultier will leave a legacy
that is both aesthetic and political. There is
no boundary for him between masculinity and
femininity. What interests him is the ambiguity
of the sexes, the mixing of the genders.'

FARIDA KHELFA

'HE HAD A WONDERFUL SENSE OF PLAYFULNESS.'

MARIAN MCEVOY, WOMEN'S WEAR DAILY

'FASHION EDITORS CALL HIS CLOTHES
CLOSET CLASSICS. THE DRAMA AND
TAWDRY EXUBERANCE OF HIS FASHION
SHOWS OBSCURE THEIR BASIS IN DEFT
COAT AND JACKET TAILORING.'

GEORGINA HOWELL, VOGUE

CLOSET CLASSICS

Ultimately, Jean Paul Gaultier's success lies in the consistency of his (classic) house codes: the deconstructed trench coat, the perfectly cut blazer, those shades of boudoir pink, a matelot sweater (inextricably linked to the designer himself) which have been constantly refreshed. For all the media-grabbing headlines surrounding his outré, daring catwalk exuberance and corsets there lie, beneath sensationally cut wardrobe classics that have always been very much part of his design vernacular. Jackets with extraordinary tailoring, trousers, skirts and dresses as sublimely cut as they are always witty. His rigorous couture training provided a powerful foundation under the drama of his clothes. They were constants that Gaultier always sought to include in his shows – in both couture and ready to wear. In fact, these classics are the very chic and much-emulated – at least in England at any rate – design staples which have come to epitomise the much-coveted uniform of the quintessential Parisienne, endlessly presented each season by designers today such as Isabel Marant and a rash of mid-price French brands.

Elevated wardrobe staples epitomise the Parisienne's quintessential day-to-day look. A model wears Gaultier's signature stripe matelot sweater, classically tailored coat and masculine tailored, gold sequined trousers from the Les Sirènes *couture collection for spring/summer 2008. Photograph by Chris Moore.*

Like Yves Saint Laurent before him, Gaultier looked to make them his own. His trench coats may have been classic in their choice of khaki or black and in the mould of the Forties' vamp, but they were often deconstructed with his signature wit and humour. Epaulettes were exaggerated, yokes contained peek-a-boo pleats and evening styles had trains that trailed the floor like ball gowns. Jackets and coats were nearly always presented with strong, sharp shoulders and waists were emphasised. In his hands, traditionally masculine tailoring could also look the height of feminine sophistication. Like the matelot stripe, Gaultier knew that all these staples, which were endlessly re-interpreted, would work in any wardrobe and never go out of style.

Georgina Howell recalled in American *Vogue*, 'At the Galerie Vivienne shop, I was encouraged to examine the clothes on the hanger itself and discovered that without the usual hype and the pretty boys, the clothes were indeed impeccably made and even justified Gaultier's perennial claim of being obsessed by traditional tailoring.

Backstage at Gaultier's show: models wear matelot sweaters, an item inextricably linked to the designer. He recalls that his mother would dress him up in sailor-striped sweaters. 'They go with everything', he told Vogue, 'they never go out of style and probably never will'. Photograph by Andrew Lamb.

Overleaf Patrick Demarchelier photographs a model about to cross the Rue de Rivoli, Paris, oozing glamour in a silk taffeta dress with a criss-cross bodice and teamed with leather wrist gloves.

Pages 126-127 Stella Tennant exudes beautifully understated androgyny (left) – the sort that Gaultier has always been keen to portray – in a wool and leather single-breasted coat, chunky polo-neck knit and tweed trousers which demonstrate Gaultier's skillful tailoring. Photograph by Nathaniel Goldberg. Gaultier uses symmetry, proportion and expert tailoring in bold, primary colours (right) to create a youthful, sporty spin on classic separates. Photograph by Josh Olins.

'I CAN SAY I AM DOING FASHION MY OWN WAY.'

JEAN PAUL GAULTIER

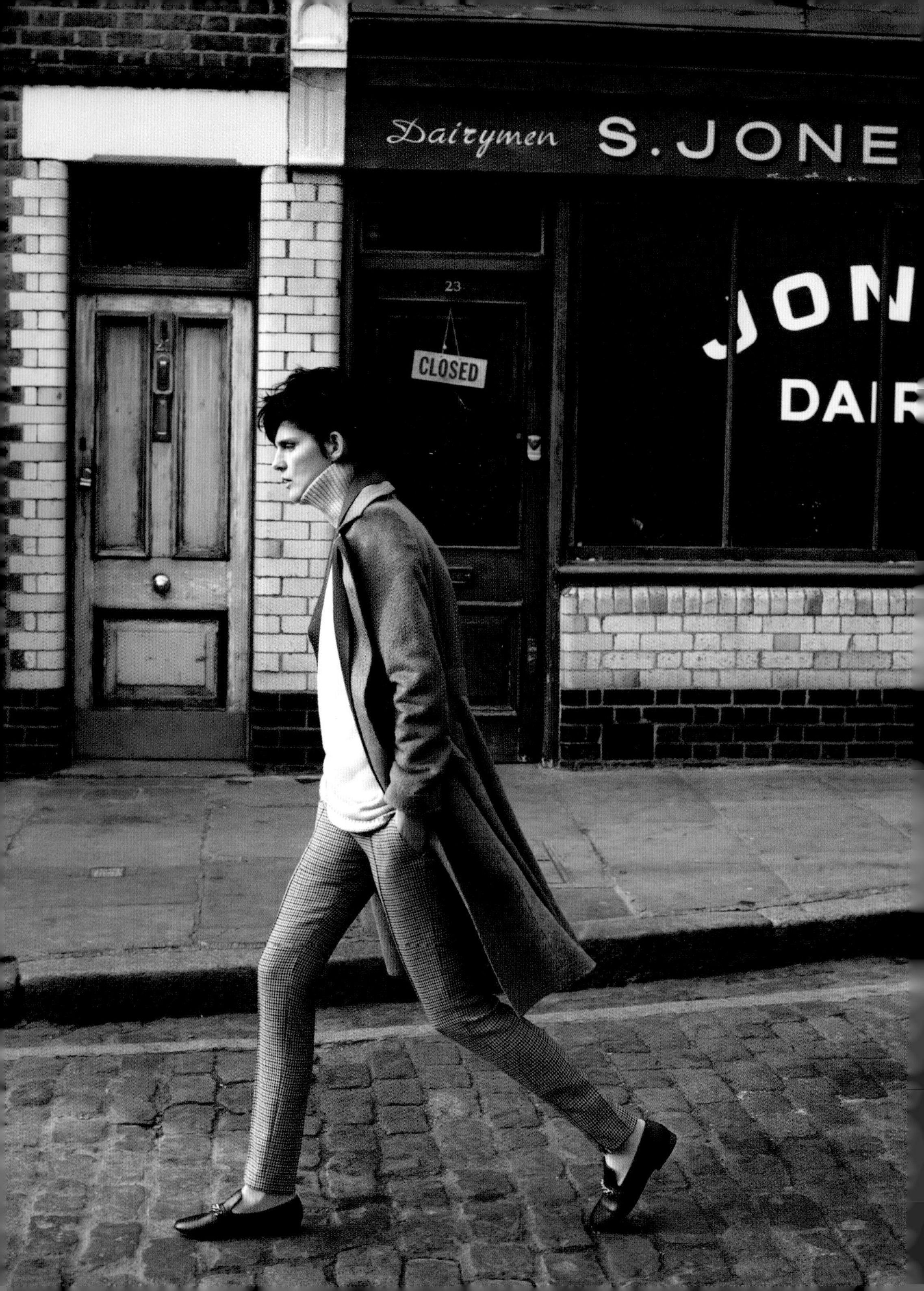
Dairymen S.JONE
23
CLOSED
JON
DAIR

Fashion editors call his clothes closet classics. The drama and tawdry exuberance of his fashion shows obscure their basis in deft coat and jacket tailoring.'

I t is no accident that these were the defining characteristics of the quintessential Parisienne's uniform. 'The Parisienne is the woman I know best.' Gaultier told *Vogue*, 'but it's also possible I still haven't actually met her ... I've designed many runway shows both for my haute couture and ready-to-wear around the theme of Paris and its female icons and characters, monuments and neighbourhoods. It was Jacques Becker's [Paris-set] film *Falbalas* that made me first want to become a designer.'

When the minimalist Nineties swept in, Gaultier was able to embrace the fashion readily since his house codes already incorporated the staples of a stylish Frenchwoman's uniform. His sharply tailored trench, tuxedo trousers and striped sweater have provided a style template for legions of women who adopted Gallic chic with its rakish air of insouciance that has proved still popular long after the turn of the millennium.

Gaultier's Paris brings the feel of the city of the Belle Époque or the interwar years back to life: Parisians like Toulouse Lautrec and La Goulue, corner bistros and pavement cafés, the figures in the Brassaï photographs from the 1930s, a cocky irreverence. Like the heroine of that most Parisian of films, *Amélie*, he loves the postcard Paris of the Eiffel Tower, the Folies Bergère, the bars and theatres of Pigalle and the colourful throngs crowding the streets of the Barbès area.

In his spring/summer 1988 collection, Gaultier's Parisienne wears a beret and has a cigarette stuck in her mouth; by his spring/summer 1995 collection, she is an elegant fin-de-siècle siren. In a silver-fox stole worn over a pinstriped suit worthy of a 1930s pimp. *Parisianizes* is the Gaultier woman for autumn/winter 2010. She morphs into a 1940s existentialist (autumn/winter 1982) a 1950s couture customer (haute couture spring/summer 1997) or a 1970s punk (spring/summer 1997).

'DRESSING IS A PLEASURE. CLOTHES ARE NOT A JOKE'

JEAN PAUL GAULTIER

Arthur Elgort photographs Gaultier bringing a playful, streetwise attitude to couture. Adorned in strands of diamanté and an ostrich-feather hat, Karen Elson wears an Aran cable-stitched top and crocheted skirt over sumptuous layers of tulle for a modern version of the style of the Belle Époque.

The Gaultier Paris autumn/winter 1992 was a veritable tribute to the city of Jean Paul Sartre and Juliette Gréco. As Lisa Armstrong, *Vogue*'s fashion features director during the Nineties remembers, 'Even though many of his favourite tropes are what we think of as British – trench coats, Savile Row – I think there is something ineffably French about them. It's to do with the way he tailored masculine clothes for women and made them very feminine. It's Charlotte Rampling or Jane Birkin isn't it? Ironically, they're British too, but with French polish and angles. That gender fluidity seems commonplace now, but it was much more rare in the 80s, and there were very few places a woman could go to get androgynous clothes that would actually flatter her shape and looked seductive.'

In 2000, Gaultier produced one of his most dazzling love letters to Paris by paying homage in his couture collection to the spirit of Paris by night. The dress, featured in *Vogue*, was a design taken from an aerial photograph of the Pigalle quarter in the Thirties. It was sketched by Gaultier and then printed onto silk velvet. The work involved a team of specialist embroiderers, using over 10,000 sequins in 31 styles (the 'glowing' neon posed a particular challenge), to hand-stitch the cityscape onto the fabric. The dress was hand-lined in silk and took 360 hours to make.

In this collection Gaultier turned his imagination to the classic icons of Paris – its architecture, the lights of Pigalle, the legendary nightlife characters – and translated them into stunning 'pop' couture Thus, a simple tweed dress decorated with black wool embroidery became a portrait of the interwar model, singer and artist Kiki de Montparnasse, while a mermaid-tailed sheath covered with shaded green sequins appeared to flicker with a pixelated image of a kissing couple. He even tackled the city's premier attraction – the Eiffel Tower – which became a remarkable bronze dress encased in a layer of crochet which evoked the complex iron construction.

Gaultier's homage to Paris continued with the nonchalant elegance of a black lace spider-web cape, feathered headpiece and the sultry yet classic appeal of a cut-on-the-bias pale silk jersey dress. Photograph by Mario Testino.

Overleaf *Corinne Day shows the 1990s 'made-under' style (left) with Gaultier's transparent golden mesh tunic worn over a nautical stripe t-shirt dress. Gaultier's poetic tatters of tulle and lace (right): model Angela Lindvall wears a white silk tulle and velvet corset dress while Frankie Rayder wears a pale pink lacy strapless tulle tiered evening gown. Photograph by Nick Knight.*

The classic Gaultier sailor top was a combination of many things but first and foremost a childhood memory. He recalls that his mother would dress him up in sailor-striped sweaters. 'They go with everything,' he told *Vogue*, 'they never go out of style and probably never will. There were also other influences: my grandmother, Coco Chanel, Jean Genet, Popeye, [the homoerotic artist] Tom of Finland, Rainer Fassbinder and his film *Querelle*. When I started in fashion, I'd already adopted the sailor striped sweater as my uniform; that way I wouldn't have to drive myself crazy trying to figure out what to wear. I wore it with a kilt, leather trousers, my men's skirt, a tuxedo. I've worked variations of stripes and the sailor uniform in to each of my haute couture and prêt-à-porter collections and in all possible and impossible materials from leather, feather, lace, crochet and more.'

Gaultier perfumes in containers instantly recognisable as symbolic of the designer's signature looks. The bottle for Classique, his first women's fragrance, displays an etched corset on a voluptuous female figure, while for his equally successful men's fragrance, Le Male's torso wears his matelot sweater.

***Overleaf** Mario Testino captures Gaultier's dreamy couture vision from* Les Indes Galantes *for spring/summer 2000. His bride wears a cloud of heavenly chiffon and tulle which is knotted and twisted to stunning effect.*

The stripe sweater even appeared on Le Male, his male perfume which, twenty years after its launch in 1995, is still the seventh-best-selling men's fragrance in the UK. This followed the phenomenal success of his female perfume, Le Classique, which launched in 1993 and broke records by taking $300,000 in its first week of trading at New York department store Saks Fifth Avenue. A floral oriental scent, Classique was the famous 'bust in a tin can' and has sold more than 60 million bottles since it was launched. The fragrance, which was created by perfumer Jacques Cavallier, was housed in a distinctive bottle, designed to astonish: a female torso dressed in a corset, a tribute to Gaultier's maternal grandmother. Its designers were inspired by the bottle shape of the Elsa Schiaparelli perfume Shocking which, when it came out in 1937, evoked Mae West's generous curves. The bottle came in a metal can, a nod to Andy Warhol's prints and to Gaultier's bracelets from his earliest shows which were fashioned from old tins. 'The success of a scent is a lottery,' Pierre Dinand, the respected perfume bottle designer, told *Vogue* in 1993. 'Without a distinctive bottle it will be very hard to win.'

'MY HAUTE COUTURE DREAM IS HAUTE COUTURE THAT SELLS.'

JEAN PAUL GAULTIER

Gaultier has taken many risks, often stepping outside of the accepted trajectory of a designer's career and, although this has excited many and has contributed to his fame, his reputation has sometimes suffered for this. There was the 1989 dance single titled 'Aow Tou Dou Zat', a sound collage that he recorded with the English producer Tony Mansfield and which took as its starting point excerpts from a 1997 BBC interview with the designer. It also included a mix by Norman Cook (Fatboy Slim) and ended up in the Top 100 in the European dance charts. The CD cover featured a stylised photograph of Gaultier, his hair in full spike, a puckish smile on his face.

In 1993 he became a television presenter on the British TV show *Eurotrash*, a satirical romp through the wilder extremes of contemporary European popular culture. Co-hosted by Antoine de Caunes and broadcast on Fridays at 11pm, it was essential Friday evening television and enjoyed peak viewing figures of around two to three million. Although the show was an undoubted hit and authentically reflected Gaultier's eclectic creative inspirations, it almost certainly deprived him of the opportunity to take up the mantle at Christian Dior.

Bernard Arnault, boss of Dior's owners LVMH, was apparently not amused by *Eurotrash*. Gaultier said he had been approached to discuss the job of producing ready-to-wear and couture collections two years before John Galliano was appointed to be creative director of Christian Dior. Gaultier had been informed that Arnault disliked his association with Eurotrash, feeling that it was inconsistent with the importance of the role at Dior. He was also secretly told that it was felt that it would be an embarrassment if, as design director at Dior, he ever had to meet the Princess of Wales – although, as Gaultier tells Colin McDowell, he had also been secretly told that the Princess of Wales often watched *Eurotrash*.

Even ten years earlier, when Christian Lacroix left the house of Jean Patou, Gaultier had suggested to Patou that a group of designers including Claude Montana, Thierry Mugler, Azzedine Alaïa, Vivienne Westwood and Romeo Gigli might all take turns to produce a couture show. As he explained to McDowell, 'We were all pretty much working to couture standards. It would have been perfectly possible as Patou did not really have a house style. It didn't have the strong personality of Dior or Saint Laurent. So each designer could have done a collection per season. Patou's immediate response? "Too expensive". They didn't even consider it. That is *so* French. We weren't even asking for money!'

Arnault suggested that Gaultier take Galliano's place at Givenchy. Gaultier told *Vogue*. 'I thought Givenchy was very bourgeois ... I loved Saint Laurent. Dior. Cardin. Givenchy was not a dream of mine. So I told Mr Arnault no. I was not dreaming of Givenchy. More than 4000 people were coming to my shows: why would I design for anyone else other than Dior? That's when I felt the urge to open up my own couture house, under my own name. Some people would buy an apartment rather than plunge into such an adventure. Not me. Right from the first collection we had orders, and we immediately started on the next one.' So, as Francis Menuge had suggested many years earlier, he started his own haute couture line: this was an antidote to *Eurotrash*, and his consolation for not getting the Dior job.

In 1997, Gaultier opened his own couture house, becoming only the third designer in three decades (after Lacroix and Mugler) to create couture under his own label. Some of his most creative and praised collections have occurred in that time. From a strapless, feather-enhanced denim ball gown to a seashell-bodiced dress with a feather-covered skirt, he has won a reputation for clothing combining outrageous features with high-quality tailoring and detailing. Unlike other couture houses that work only with toiles, Gaultier prefers to directly sculpt the particular material that he envisions for a specific outfit – or a material similar to it – in order to get an exact idea of the possible volumes and effects.

The haute couture clothes that he had dreamt so much of as a child had become a reality. 'I wanted to do everything by the book, such as devising shows without music,' he told *Vogue*. 'For my first couture show, presented in a trompe l'oeil salon setting, the film critic Élisabeth Quin announced each outfit by name and number as the models came out, the way it used to be done.' But despite his decorous, traditional presentation, his haute couture collections were created for the modern client. 'My runway shows don't serve to promote my brand or decorate red carpets. My haute couture dream is haute couture that sells.' 'Everyone wondered what he would produce in the rarefied area of craftsmanship,' recalls Carine Roitfeld. 'He caused a shock by presenting a really classic haute couture show, with each outfit having a number that was announced as the model walked down the runway, as had been the custom in the past.'

By the mid-Nineties, the number of couture customers was dwindling and there was a feeling that the business was decadent, and fading. Lisa Armstrong says, 'I think we were all quite surprised, in so far as couture was meant to be dying and no one could see how it could be sustainable without a big backer behind it. But couture seems to have been dying for 50 years, and there are plenty of couturiers that are doing very nicely. I think all creative designers ultimately dream of having their own label where money and commercial objectives aren't the only motivation.'

Vogue enthusiastically covered his couture collections, which were regularly described as ravishing. His 2001 January collection was particularly notable for its Belle-Époque bohemians, Moulin-Rouge hedonists and sport – a cocktail only Gaultier could pull off. Tailoring was sliced and slashed to reveal skin on his renditions of the little black dress and Le Smoking; his signature trench was transformed with cut-out black panels, and knitted sheath minidresses featured swags of crystal-encrusted yarn looping down bare backs. The 'worn' and 'torn' decoration was pure dynamite, allowing flashes of skin to peep through. In 2000 he received an International Award from the Council of Fashion designers of America. In 2001 he was named a Chevalier of the National Order of the Legion of Honour, and in 2002 the Paris boutique on the Avenue George V opened.

Mario Testino depicts Gaultier's ongoing love affair with lingerie, perhaps a throwback to his childhood when he spent hours rummaging through his grandmother's undergarments. A model wears a black mini-dress covered in swags of crystal-encrusted yarn.

Overleaf *Audrey Marnay wears Gaultier's finely crafted, 'Fin-de-Siecle' long beaded slip dress with fringed layers and hem (left), an outfit that references the designer's appreciation for Belle Époque exuberance. Photograph by Mario Testino. Arthur Elgort captures Lily Cole (right) in a metallic headpiece and sequined gold and silver cape, a product of the often fantastical element of Gaultier's escapist imagination.*

Meanwhile Gaultier's design influence had also extended to film, something he had always been passionate about. He designed the wardrobe of many films including Luc Besson's *The Fifth Element*, for which he was nominated for a César Award for best costume design, Pedro Almodovar's *Kika*, *Bad Education* and *The Skin I Live in*, Peter Greenaway's *The Cook, the Thief, His Wife & Her Lover* and Marc Caro's and Jean-Pierre Jeunet's *The City of Lost Children* for which he was also nominated for a César in 1996.

In 1999 Hermès purchased 35 per cent in Gaultier for $23.1 million. He was appointed creative director at Hermès in 2003 where he remained till 2010. As Roger Tredre and Brenda Polan have observed, contrary to what many may have thought, the distance between Gaultier (maverick, daring soul) and the classic house of Hermès wasn't so great. In interviews he recalled the comment of Helmut Newton, who joked that Hermès is the most important sex shop in the world with its leather, whips and stirrups. Inès de la Fressange said, 'I understand why Hermès chose him as its designer and artistic director: he has a classical line and elegant style, and he has a feeling for materials. You sense that he approached his duties with immense respect for the heritage of that great house.' Valerie Steele meanwhile believed that Hermès had 'chosen him because it wanted someone with a very strong vision who could push the brand out of its bourgeois ghetto and into more fashion-forward territory. Hermès is synonymous with leather, and in Gaultier, whose designs reflected a radical sensibility, they found the ideal person for exploiting all the perverse sexuality of the material. Moreover, the fact that he was an outstanding couturier, with a mastery of cut and materials, made him a perfect fit for Hermès, whose reputation has been built on quality of design and craftsmanship.'

Taking the theme of 'underwear as outerwear' to extremes, actress Milla Jovovich's startling 'bandage dress' bodysuit was perhaps the most shocking of Gaultier's striking and much-admired costumes for Luc Besson's 1997 film The Fifth Element.

'Perfection is relative and beauty is subjective.'

JEAN PAUL GAULTIER

In recent years, Gaultier has also had his setbacks: his only boutique in the United States, on Madison Avenue, closed in 2005 and like many labels battling with the recession at the beginning of the Noughties (as well as, in his case, the pressure of maintaining a couture operation) he had to make job cuts in 2004 after orders dropped. In 2008, Hermès increased their stake to 45 per cent, becoming the largest investors, until they sold their stake in 2011 to Puig: it was the first time since Gaultier launched his label that an investor has held a majority stake.

Gaultier is one of the rare couturiers who has spent four decades in perpetual evolution, in search of the new, season after season, but in 2014 he announced that he was stopping his ready-to-wear line and would focus on couture because he felt the current state of homogenized fashion did not favour creativity. He cited the frenetic pace of fashion and the sheer number of collections a designer must create. He told *Vogue*, 'The industry has changed and people don't appreciate true craftsmanship. I think we are driving ourselves crazy with this relentless demand for new, new, new. It's got to the stage where ready-to-wear isn't about selling clothes but to represent the image of the brand. Well in that case, what is the point, we are over producing, there are more clothes than you have people who can wear them.' He explained that 'I sometimes finish off 45–60 pieces in a single fitting session. Sometimes I see designs three times in a row. At that frantic pace you have less time to reflect. Haute couture allows me to take a break until the next day, which is unthinkable in prêt-à-porter now.'

In the saddle: Gaultier photographed by Patrick Demarchelier at the Hermès workshop above the label's rue du Faubourg St Honoré store. He was creative director for the esteemed French house from 2003 until 2010.

Overleaf The model Jasmine Guinness wearing a crêpe jersey couture dress from Galerie Gaultier. For all the media-grabbing headlines that surrounded his outré, daring catwalk exuberance, there lies beneath sensationally cut classics that have always been very much part of his wardrobe vernacular. Photograph by Karen Collins.

I n 2011 an expertly created and curated exhibition, *The Fashion World of Jean Paul Gaultier: From the Sidewalk to the Catwalk*, opened at the Montreal Museum of Fine Arts. Celebrating the designer's 35-year career, the exhibition has travelled all over the world, from New York to London, from Seoul to Stockholm, and finally to Paris in 2015.

'I START EACH
COLLECTION
THINKING
HOW I CAN
REFRESH MY
CLASSICS.'

JEAN PAUL GAULTIER

In the accompanying volume to the exhibition, Thierry-Maxime Loriot has interviewed many high-profile fashion insiders who have followed Gaultier's career. The contribution of Martin Margiela, Gaultier's former design assistant from 1985–1987 (particularly moving, as Margiela's retiring, reclusive personality is so much the antithesis of the exuberant Gaultier), is perhaps the best summary of his mentor's career. 'He [Gaultier] knows how to surprise people, how to reinvent himself, how to innovate. His insatiable interest in the very many different fields proves the extent of his energy and his ability to throw himself into areas beyond fashion: he enhances choreographies through his outfits he dresses stars in movies, he designs costumes with such a strong impact that they end up personifying the artist who wears them.'

The exhibition was a celebration rather than a valediction: Gaultier had never intended that it might be considered a retrospective. 'I haven't died or gone into retirement just yet,' he told *Le Monde*. 'I don't consider myself an artist and my clothes have always been designed to be worn, not stuck behind a glass cabinet'. The exhibition has been a sell-out everywhere, attracting over two million visitors who have come to see the impressive, entertaining and diverse body of work that Gaultier has created, charting the continual evolution of street versus haute fashion during the past four decades.

Jean Paul Gaultier walks out to take his bow on the catwalk of his autumn/winter 2002 couture collection, Les Hussardes. *Photograph by Anders Overgaard.*

Overleaf *Gaultier's candy-floss pink, gently ruffled dress which falls in silk cascades evokes a 1940s glamour that has been re-imagined for the present day. Photograph by Carter Smith.*

'I am very lucky because I am realising my childhood dreams.'

JEAN PAUL GAULTIER

Index

Page numbers in *italic* refer to illustrations

References

Bolton, Andrew *Punk:Chaos to Couture (Metropolitan Museum of Art)*, Yale University Press, 2013

Chenoune, Farid *Jean Paul Gaultier (Fashion Memoir)*, Thames & Hudson, 1996

Loriot, Thierry-Maxime (ed) *The Fashion World of Jean Paul Gaultier: From the Sidewalk to the Catwalk*, Montreal: Museum of Fine Arts, 2011

McDowell, Colin *Jean Paul Gaultier*, Viking Books, 2001

Polan, Brenda and Roger Tredre *The Great Fashion Designers*, Berg, 2009

Picture credits

Acknowledgements

Many thanks to *Vogue*, especially to Harriet Wilson, Brett Croft, Carole Dumoulin, Richard Pickard, Sarah Harris and Lucinda Chambers. Sarah Mitchell for being a wonderful editor, Gemma Hayden, Jane O'Shea, Nicola Ellis, Lisa Armstrong, Laura Craik and Jelka Music at Jean Paul Gaultier.

Publishing Consultant Jane O'Shea
Creative Director Helen Lewis
Series Editor Sarah Mitchell
Series Designer Nicola Ellis
Designer Gemma Hayden
Production Director Vincent Smith
Production Controller Emily Noto

For *Vogue*:
Commissioning Editor Harriet Wilson
Picture Researcher Carole Dumoulin

First published in 2017 by
Quadrille Publishing Limited
Pentagon House
52-54 Southwark Street
London SE1 1UN
www.quadrille.co.uk

Text copyright © 2017 Condé Nast
Publications Limited
Vogue Regd TM is owned by the Condé
Nast Publications Ltd and is used under
licence from it. All rights reserved.

Design and layout © 2017 Quadrille
Publishing Limited

Quadrille is an imprint of Hardie Grant
www.hardiegrant.com.au

Cataloguing in Publication Data: a
catalogue record for this book is
available from the British Library.

ISBN 978 184949 969 9

Printed in China